Claudia Williams

Robert Meyrick

Llyfrgell Genedlaethol Cymru • National Library of Wales
Aberystwyth 2000

Llyfrgell Genedlaethol Cymru • National Library of Wales

Aberystwyth 2000

A publication to coincide with a retrospective touring exhibition of Claudia Williams' work starting at the National Library of Wales, Aberystwyth.

ISBN 1 86225 018 9

Acknowledgements

I am indebted to D. Michael Francis and Huw Ceiriog Jones at the National Library of Wales for their support of this exhibition and publication and to Neil Holland for reading the manuscript and offering valuable suggestions. I am especially grateful Claudia Williams and Gwilym Prichard for their encouragement, friendship and for allowing me unlimited access to their studios and personal archive of press cuttings. It has been a delight to come to know them.

Photographs by Rudy Lewis, Robert Meyrick, Gwilym Prichard and the National Library of Wales.

Front Cover: *Mothers on the Beach* 1986, oil on canvas 91.5 x 122 cm, Private Collection, France

Title Page: Claudia Williams, Rochefort-en-Terre, January 1998 (Photograph: Robert Meyrick)

Designed & Printed by Cambrian Printers, Aberystwyth

Claudia Williams

The unprecedented interest in contemporary Welsh painting and reappraisal of the visual arts in Wales in recent years has created a resurgence of interest in the generation of figurative artists whose careers came to the fore during the post-war period. Husband and wife Gwilym Prichard and Claudia Williams lived in Wales until 1984 and in France until Spring 2000. They now divide their time between properties in Rochefort-en-Terre in Brittany and Tenby. Prichard and Williams are passionate about painting, for them art and life are neatly dovetailed; they work around each other's needs in the studio and at home, and they have been fortunate to earn a living doing what they enjoy most. Both artists have exhibited widely in Europe and despite years of self-imposed exile on the Continent they have staged numerous group and solo exhibitions in Wales. Their paintings have a popular appeal and they are represented in public collections in Britain and private collections world wide.

Family life has been an enduring theme for Claudia Williams, all her paintings have been based on human relationships and figures in close proximity. For her family life and her activities as a painter have been inseparable. Even when the children were very young and it was not possible to concentrate on painting for sustained periods of time, she filled sketchbooks with drawings that would later become an invaluable resource for paintings. She has always acknowledged the limitations imposed by her domestic circumstances, for her they provided

1.
Claudia Williams aged 15

the perfect opportunity for a harmonious integration of art and life. The lives of both painters have also complemented one another; at times of financial hardship, personal difficulties and illness they have ably reconciled family life and their careers as artists.

Since childhood Claudia Williams has drawn and painted those around her, creating what are in some respects visual diaries of her family and friends. At home, women and children perform their daily routine and provide an opportunity for paintings that focus on social interaction. She has also been drawn to the sea, and the beach has been a rich subject for depicting figures in groups. Williams has a particular sensibility towards the human condition, to gesture and facial expression. This perceptiveness is manifest in her many paintings that employ flattened spatial recession and formalised organisation of two-dimensional space. Her compositions display an inherent sense of design, sensitive handling of colour and confident figure drawing.

Claudia Jane Herington Williams was born in Purley, Surrey in 1933 the great-grand daughter of a Cardiganshire sheep farmer. She is the only child of Frank Williams, a London-born civil servant, and his wife Gladys Irene, née Herington of Leicester. In September 1938, when 5 years old, Claudia became a day pupil at Eothen School for Girls in the Harestone Valley near Caterham. In 1941 mother and daughter moved to Devon for a year away from the bombing around London. Here she began school as a weekly boarder at the Convent of the Assumption in Sidmouth where in May that year her artistic abilities were recognised when she was awarded The Drawing Society Certificate. Her mother lived in various boarding houses in Devon but after a year they returned to the austerity of war-time London; to a city of air raids, doodle bugs and severe food rationing. Frank Williams was not a robust man, he had experienced the trenches during World War I, and now there were additional duties at the office after hours and fire watching at the Ministry of Health. In spite of this, Claudia's parents stressed the importance of a good education and sacrificed luxuries for her schooling, she was encouraged to be creative and was also sent for lessons in piano and dance. She took the Royal Academy of Dancing Children's Examinations in 1943 and 1944. After the war her parents moved to Llangybi near Chwilog on the Lleyn Peninsula and in 1946 they retired there permanently. Here they came to know John Petts and Jonah Jones who were running the small Caseg Press at Llanystumdwy and both encouraged Claudia with her artwork.

In 1947 Claudia won second prize in an art competition organised for the BBC's Welsh Children's Hour. The Award not only fuelled her interest in art but she then became intent upon pursuing a career in art. In September that year, after an unhappy term at the local school, she returned to Eothen as a boarder. Here, she was fortunate to benefit once more from the enthusiasm and encouragement of Christine Walker, a brilliant art mistress who had been a student of Graham Sutherland. Walker paid special attention to her imaginative and resourceful pupil. She encouraged her delight in narrative picture making, especially Claudia's interest in hand-made books, illustrated with lively ink drawings and brightly coloured poster paints. Her book *Monsters* is

> a collection of poems and descriptions about living and imaginary things, things seen on the earth and things that are purely fantastic, creatures that I have conjured up in my mind as monsters and insects that no eye has ever seen before.[1]

In this book, Claudia's own stories are interspersed with extracts from a variety of texts: John Bunyon's *Pilgrim's Progress,* Lewis Carrol's *Jabberwocky,* Edward Lear's *The Dong with a Luminous Nose,* Walter de la Mare's *Ride by Nights,* John Milton's *Paradise Lost* and Percy

---

1. CW, foreword *Monsters* 1949.

2.
Milking
1949
ink on paper
dimensions and
present
whereabouts
unknown

3.
Park Scene
1952
oil on canvas
50 x 61 cm
The Artist

4.
Family on the Beach
1957
oil on board
77.5 x 102 cm
The Artist

5.
Girls with Siamese Cats
1961
oil on board
61 x 84 cm
Private Collection, UK

Bysshe Shelley's *Ozymandias*. Another hand-made book, *Heard in a Raid,* illustrated in monochrome ink and wash contains a

> collection of stories some of which are fantastic and imaginary while others are stories that I have been told by people who have travelled and seen curious things.[2]

In *The Wild Adventures of Daring Dick* she tells of the life of an eleven year old boy in a circus, his mother is an acrobat and his father a clown. Dick is a bare-back rider who performs with his horse Silver and his monkey Lollypop.

Always a prolific and spirited letter writer, many of Claudia's letters to her parents have survived. In them she tells of her work in the art studios, news of her friends, and anticipation of a 'horsey half-term' visiting the local horse shows (Plate 1). Accounts of packed lunches in the countryside, the first cherries and strawberries of the season, and bicycle rides to Ashdown Forest or the racecourse at Epsom conjure images of idyllic, 'Swallows and Amazons' childhood summers.

---

2. CW, foreword *Heard in a Raid* 1949.

6.
Mothers at Breakfast
1963
oil on board
82 x 56 cm
Private
Collection, UK

7.
On the Garden Path
1963
oil on board
Dimensions unknown
Private Collection, UK

8.
*Children with
Tricycles*
1964
oil on board
51 x 61 cm
Private
Collection, UK

In one undated letter, Claudia writes to her parents

> During the weekend we both worked extremely hard, and had a lot of our meals in the studio. I did three
> paintings this weekend, the third one is of a woman washing up.[3]

In July 1949 this picture was included along with three others in the National Exhibition of Children's Art at the Royal Institute Galleries in Piccadilly. The competition was open to all schools in the country and there were nearly 47,000 entries of which 272 works were hung. The exhibition toured to Manchester, Leeds, Bristol and Newcastle, and a selection was sent to the United States. The distinguished judges Philip James (Director of Art, Arts Council of Great Britain), John Rothenstein (Director of the Tate Gallery) and Herbert Read (President of the Society for Education through Art) were unanimous in their decision to give the principal award to Claudia Williams for the picture *Milking* (Plate 2). She received the *Sunday Pictorial* Art Training Scholarship, a bursary worth two hundred and fifty pounds. (Eothen was the only school to have two pupils in the final; her school friend Shirley Blomfield came second and was to win the prize the following year.) Claudia's entries *Washing Up* and *Girl Knitting* anticipate a later preoccupation with domestic scenes and family life.

---

3. CW, letter to her parents, probably Spring 1949.

9.
Mrs Dawkins
1978
oil on canvas
76 x 51 cm
The Artist

Isn't it simply marvellous? Emma sent for Blom and me yesterday morning and we went up expecting a row until we saw her face! She was chuckling away and we couldn't think what on earth it was. She flourished a letter in our faces, and I can't remember what she said, but we just stood there absolutely dazed, which she read out that Claudia's and Shirley's paintings are among the best sent in and they are among the final runners up for the £250 prize.[4]

Both pupils were awarded three guineas each for art materials and the School twenty pounds for the art room. The exhibition was opened by George Strauss MP, Minister of Supply. He was pleased with the standard of entries but feared

far too many of these children, when they leave school, give up exercising their imaginative talent because they think it is looked upon as something queer or even sissy.[5]

Claudia was invited to take part in a Pathé newsreel about the *Sunday Pictorial* competition and a television report at the BBC studios at Alexander Palace. Christine Walker was her escort to London.

---

4. CW, undated letter to her parents.
5. George Strauss *Sunday Pictorial,* 4 September 1949.

10.
*Mother on the
Beach*
1970s
oil on canvas
92 x 61.5 cm
Private
Collection, UK

Claudia Williams completed her studies for the School Leaving Certificate at Eothen and
the Training Award was held over for a year. At the age of sixteen, and following in the
footsteps of her art teacher, she attended Chelsea School of Art between 1950 to 1953. Her
tutors included Raymond Coxon, Bernard Meadows, Frances Richards and Julian Trevelyan.
The most valuable experience for her at Chelsea she remembers was the life class under

11.
Bedsitter II
1981
oil on board
61 x 81 cm
National Library of
Wales

12.
Collecting Shells
1981
oil on canvas
61 x 122 cm
National Library
of Wales

the tutelage of the sculptor Bernard Meadows, who had been a student of Henry Moore. 'I used to love those life-drawing lessons', she recalled, 'getting everything to look really solid. And that's never left me, really.'[6] Maybe the sturdy sculptural forms of her paintings of women on the beach and mothers with their babies were inherited indirectly from Moore. At Chelsea, Williams was awarded the Christopher Head Scholarship for Drawing. In August 1951 she received the 'Special Certificate of Merit' from *The Newcastle Sun* for

---

6. CW, interview with Ian Skidmore, BBC Radio Wales, 1985.

13.
Family with Oranges
c.1982
oil on board
91.5 x 122 cm
Private Collection, UK

her work and in 1952 *Park Scene* was her first contribution to the National Eisteddfod of Wales (Plate 3).

After Chelsea, Williams returned to north Wales where she married the young painter Gwilym Prichard in 1954. Prichard was born in Llanystumdwy, near Criccieth in 1931 and trained at Birmingham School of Art. He is principally a painter of the Romantic-Picturesque landscape of Cader Idris, Tan-y-Grisiau and the upland and coastal regions of north Wales but he has also been drawn to the landscapes of Brittany, Provence, Italy, Greece and Tunisia. Their first home was on the Isle of Anglesey where they lived above a newsagent's shop until the birth of their first child when they moved into a council house at Pencraig, Llangefni. They had four children, Ceri, Benjamin, Justin and Clare and they worked hard as parents and painters, enduring considerable financial hardship as a consequence. Prichard taught art and craft at Llangefni Comprehensive School to support the family and sales of pictures supplemented their income. He undertook his share of the housework and attended to the children in order that Williams was able to paint and continue to exhibit. When her children were young her mother was also nearby to lend a hand.

After the children were bathed and tucked up in bed they set to work in a shared studio in the cramped front room of the house. From the outset their domestic circumstances attracted the attention of the press. This is reflected in exhibition reviews of the late 1950s with headlines that run 'Artist-mother stages her first solo exhibition', 'After the children are put to bed', 'They made 100 paintings in their council house', 'It's art in a council house for two' and

14.
*Madonna and
Child and Beach
Children*
1983
oil on board
183 x 122 cm
The Artist

15.
*Family by the
Breakwater*
1983
oil on board
91.5 x 122 cm
Private
Collection, UK

'Happy ending to six month's hard labour: 110 paintings made in the front room of a council house'. In spite of the constraints of raising a young family, Williams exhibited fifty-four paintings in her first solo show at the Tegfryn Gallery in Menai Bridge. She was also a regular contributor to exhibitions organised by the Howard Roberts Gallery in Cardiff, the Welsh Arts Council, Society for Education through Art at the National Museum of Wales and the National Eisteddfod of Wales.

Williams embarked upon a painting career at a time when the figurative tradition was still acclaimed in Wales.[7] In 1957 her painting *Family by the Sea,* which includes portraits of Gwilym Prichard and baby Benjamin, was runner up for the Gold Medal at the National Eisteddfod at Llangefni (Plate 4). The judges Ceri Richards, C.F. Tunnicliffe and Stephen Bone awarded the Gold Medal to George Chapman for his *View in Merthyr Tydfil,* announcing that they

---

7. For a background to the visual arts in the post-war years and the opportunities that existed for artists to exhibit in Wales, see Robert Meyrick *John Elwyn* National Library of Wales Press, Aberystwyth 1996.

16.
Peace Vigil
1984
oil on board
184 x 123 cm
National Library
of Wales

17.
Greek Memories
1985
oil on canvas
97 x 130 cm
The Artist

18.
Women in Greece II
1985
oil on canvas
91.5 x 122 cm
Private Collection, UK

would have awarded another medal if one were available for the best general standard by an artist showing more than one picture. It would have gone to Claudia Williams.[8]

In 1958 they moved to Old Bank House in Church Street, Beaumaris. Williams' young family confined her to many hours at home where she took the opportunity to draw and paint her children and their friends, recording their development as they grew up from babies.

When painting portraits with children I make lots of quick sketches with the children, if they are young, playing around me. I try to make it fun for them, sketching them in their own surroundings, completely relaxed and natural. When I go home I work out the general design, taking one child at a time.[9]

8. Unmarked newspaper cutting from CW.
9. *Herefordshire Life,* March 1976.

19.
Claudia Williams
1986

20.
*Christmas
Presents*
1986
oil on canvas
91.5 x 122 cm
The Artist

In carefully structured compositions, unusually observed from a high vantage point, the
young children are totally preoccupied with their activities – earnestly cutting paper
patterns, kneeling over a painting, stroking the Siamese cats or sprawled cross the carpet
absorbed in a book (Plate 5). The steeply elevated ground level accentuates the patterns
made by the children's bodies, minimises the need for perspective and topples the viewer
into the child's world of paper cut outs, crayons, toys and tricycles (Plate 8). Williams
captures their awkwardness, innocence and initial attempts at sociability with great integrity.

21.
Reveur sur la Plage
1986
oil on canvas
73 x 92 cm
Private
Collection, UK

Never are her paintings of children sentimentalised, nor does she attempt representational accuracy in her search for the essential form, gesture and character of the young children. Williams' paintings are very much the product of intense feeling and caring for the subject. In *Mothers at Breakfast* (1963), for example, the painted surface of warm reds, ochre, white and greys is textural and spontaneous in its application, with much of the under-painting remaining exposed. Form is suggested by the subtle modulation of the broken black outline (Plate 6). Her very distinct formalisation was in part indebted to Pablo Picasso but, closer to home, she also admired the work of Brenda Chamberlain whom she visited on Bardsey Island as a teenager.

In 1962 the Marchioness of Anglesey saw her work and commissioned a portrait group of her three children in the informal surroundings of the playroom at Plas Newydd. Since then other portrait commissions have followed for adults and/or children, single or group portraits. These include the Welsh composer Professor William Mathias in 1974, Louis Bleriot in 1989 and later that year the Jesuits at St Beuno's Monastery at St Asaph commissioned a painting to celebrate the centenary of the birth of the poet Gerald Manley Hopkins.

22.
La Plage le Soir
1986
oil on canvas
100 x 81 cm
Private
Collection, France

23.
Le Petit Dejeuner
1986
oil on canvas
91.5 x 122 cm
Private
Collection, UK

24.
After Dinner
1986
oil on canvas
91.5 x 122 cm
Private
Collection, UK

Williams has enjoyed making homes and 'feathering a nest, I think I am a very maternal person, I loved having babies, I loved that part of my life'.[10] For years she and her husband endured all the financial hardships associated with raising a large family and they sacrificed creature comforts for their art. In 1964 Prichard was appointed to teach art at Radcliffe College and they moved to Rearsby near Leicester. He held the position for little more than a year before they returned to north Wales where he had missed the landscape and the sea. Each new home they have undertaken to renovate themselves and develop the properties to suit their needs as a family and as artists. In July 1966 they camped with the children for six windswept weeks whilst work was underway on their house in Beaumaris. They lived in this property for only two years but in need of extra space they moved on once more to Rhos Cottage at Penmon Crossroads near Beaumaris. In 1976 they moved again to Plas Gwyn at Weobley in the Welsh marches, overlooking the Black Mountains, only to return to north Wales in 1979 to Bryn Môr, Llanddona, near Beaumaris. In the following year they bought Gwredog Isaf, a small holding at Rhostryfan near Caernarfon. In 1978 Williams was elected Associate Member of the Royal Cambrian Academy of Art, becoming a full Member in 1979.

When the children were grown up and away from home, painting was a full-time preoccupation for both artists; gardening and work around the home became a relaxation between long periods in the studio. She also undertook some part-time teaching at local schools and at extra-mural courses for adults. Williams wrote

> I am just trying to develop as a painter and making up for lost time when my family was young and also the years when my husband was ill and also spent time caring for an aged parent.[11]

The series of paintings based on bed-sitter life in London were painted at this time and depicts bored flatmates as they lay idling on the bed, wash at the sink, or prepare to go out for the evening (Plate 11).

In 1984 Claudia Williams visited the peace vigil at Greenham Common on several occasions to support the women and children campaigning against the deployment of US ground launched nuclear cruise missiles at the base. She made many drawings of the women and children around the campfires at the perimeter fence that eventually led to a major oil painting, *Peace Vigil* now at the National Library of Wales (Plate 16). In this and the *Madonna and Child and Beach Children* (1983) she 'expresses her deeply felt humanitarian sentiments' through the theme of motherhood.[12] Like *Peace Vigil,* the

---

10. CW, interview with Ian Skidmore, BBC Radio Wales, 1985.
11. CW, quoted in Moira Vincentelli, *Women's Art in Wales,* Mostyn Art Gallery, Llandudno 1985.
12. Moira Vincentelli, *Women's Art in Wales,* Mostyn Art Gallery, Llandudno 1985.

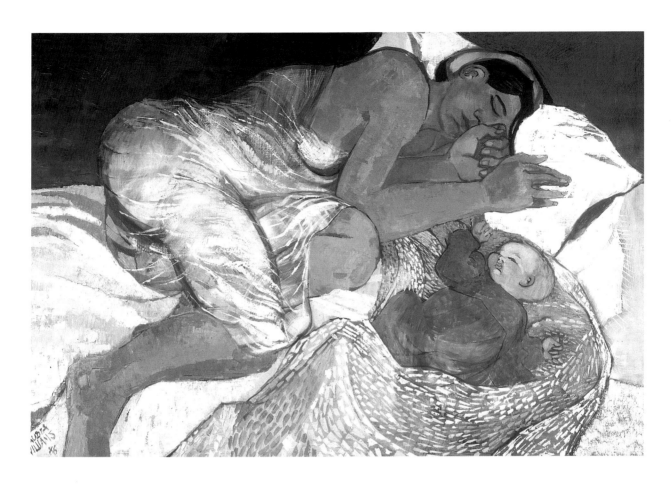

25.
Sleeping
1986
oil on canvas
73 x 92 cm
Private
Collection, France

26.
Chinese Lanterns
1987
oil on canvas
130 x 97 cm
Private
Collection, USA

27.
On the Sand
1987
oil on canvas
54 x 65 cm
The Artist

Madonna and Child and Beach Children has a triangular top and echoes the altarpiece forms used in the European tradition (Plate 14). In the symbolism of the mother and child there are strong references to Williams' Christian faith. She recalls the hours spent before Stanley Spencer's *Resurrection* at the Tate Gallery or at the National Gallery when a student at Chelsea, looking at paintings from the Italian School, especially those by Piero della Francesca.

By the time Williams reached her early fifties the cold damp climate at the foothills of Snowdonia was adversely affecting her health and making her arthritic joints ache. It persuaded them to sell their home and move to a warm, dry climate. She often refers to the 'gypsy blood' in her veins and of being stimulated by relocating to different environments, and allowing herself to metamorphose.

In 1984, when both artists had a well-established reputation in Wales, were active members of the Royal Cambrian Academy and regular exhibitors at the National Eisteddfod, they sold Gwredog Isaf. Not knowing what the future held in store, and following an old school atlas, they drove across Europe in a car laden with clothes, camping equipment and art materials. At Brindisi they crossed on the ferry to Igoumenitsa in Greece where they had been given the opportunity to look after a friend's dog, with free accommodation on the island of Skiathos for the winter.

28.
Flying Kites
1989
oil on canvas
73 x 92 cm
Private Collection, UK

29.
Sleeping Parents
1989
oil on canvas
73 x 92 cm
The Artist

In Spring, with the proceeds from the sale of a few paintings on Skiathos, they headed south to the dramatic volcanic island of Santorini. They camped in a second-hand tent and there, hunched over an old manual typewriter resting on her knees, Williams kept her travel journal up to date. She filled sketchbooks with things observed – villagers in the square on warm evenings, the men sheltering in a shady corner to avoid the heat of the afternoon sunshine,

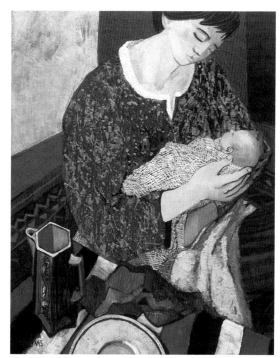

30.
Mother by the Table
1989
oil on canvas
92 x 73 cm
The Artist

31.
On the Rocks
1990
oil on canvas
50 x 61 cm
The Artist

32.
Bathers at Midnight
1990
oil on canvas
73 x 92 cm
Private Collection, France

and an old couple polishing brasses in the church in readiness for Easter. In April 1985 they made their way back through Italy, lived in a rented farmhouse surrounded by vineyards, north of St Maximin la Ste Baume in the Var, Provence, then settled in a small house near the harbour at Vannes in Brittany's Golfe de Morbihan in 1986. The sketchbook drawings in Greece, Italy and France were later worked up into oil paintings for a solo exhibition in Paris at the Galerie Romanet, Rue de Seine in October 1988 (Plate 17). Claudia Williams was awarded first prize at the Salon de Vannes in 1989 and elected a member of the Beaux Arts, Paris Salon in 1993.

In France, life continued much as it had done in Wales where they were once again forced to live frugally; this time with the satisfaction that in France, they believed there to be more general public support and interest in art and artists. In 1991 they moved inland to Rochefort-en-Terre, a quiet unspoilt medieval town of stone houses built on a rock with a population of about 650 inhabitants. Their new home on the Place de L'Eglise was formerly a boulangerie and overlooks a cobbled square across from the ancient church. Behind the town there are slate mines, albeit on a much smaller scale than the Blaenau Ffestiniog quarries to which they were accustomed, and the hills around are covered with bracken and oak trees. In that respect it was not unlike the landscape they had left behind in Wales, though they now enjoyed a temperate climate, longer daylight hours and an improved quality of light.

Rochefort-en-Terre has a long association with the visual arts. At the heart of Rochefort is the chateau that was purchased and renovated by the American painter Alfred Klots in the 1900s.

33.
The Shell
1992
oil on canvas
130 x 97 cm
Private Collection, UK

During the summer it is the home of his daughter-in-law, Isabel Klots from Baltimore, widow of Trafford Klots, the society portrait painter. The Maryland Arts Trust offers six bursaries for painters to visit the chateau and work in Brittany during the summer. Many artists from New York and Baltimore have passed through Rochefort over the years and been introduced to Prichard and Williams who have been engaged in activities organised for the visiting painters.

At Rochefort-en-Terre they work long hours alongside each other in a large, shared studio. Out of necessity they have touted their work from one gallery to another, where they have asked proprietors as far afield as Amsterdam and Paris to consider their work for a show. They have exhibited around Europe and they have been championed in the press as distinguished Welsh painters, in effect they have become ambassadors for Wales. In her studio, Williams runs figure drawing and portrait classes that are attended by students from a wide area. In 1995 Claudia Williams and Gwilym Prichard were each awarded the Silver Medal by the Academy of Arts,

34.
La Coiffeuse et Moi
1994
oil on canvas
97 x 130 cm
The Artist

35.
First Summer
1994
oil on canvas
81 x 60 cm
Private Collection, France

Sciences and Letters in Paris. They have also contributed regularly to exhibitions around Wales and are now represented by the Martin Tinney Gallery in Cardiff.

Williams observes all aspects of life around the village from the families at meal time in the cafés to the travellers passing through the village who do their laundry at the old lavoir by the river that runs alongside her garden. *La Coiffeuse et Moi* or *The Day My Hair was Cut Short* (1994) is one of numerous autobiographical paintings she has undertaken. Williams, seated bottom left, points at a fashion magazine and wonders why she does not look like the model (Plate 34).

Williams has always valued living in a beautiful landscape but, unlike her husband, she has seldom looked to landscape for a subject. Their paintings might not appear, on first

36.
Maternity
1996
pastel and diluted oil colour on paper
41 x 30.5 cm
Museum of Modern Art, Wales,
Machynlleth

impression, to share common ground. Yet in the large expanse of bed linen in *Sleeping* (1986) for example, one is suddenly aware of a landscape, the counterpane follows the contours of the reclining female form to suggest a mountainous terrain, draped over the edge of the bed it represents a beach or harbour (Plate 25). The ambiguity between what one represents and what it might also suggest appeals to Williams' imagination. Pictorial elements are inventively abstracted – alluding to, without always describing the actual body parts, gestures and postures.

In *Le Petit Dejeuner* (1986) she uses surprising and unexpected juxtapositions of colour, with flat planes of bright oranges, reds and lilac, combining opaque and transparent applications of paint which allows the under-painting to show through (Plate 23). Since the seventies her investigation of the effect of colour on the mood of the picture, has resulted in a departure from the ochre, sienna, umber and blue-greys with dominant black outline that characterise the early paintings to a more colourful palette, favouring broadly applied blues, purples, red

37.
The Race
1997
oil on canvas
122 x 65 cm
The Artist

38.
Conversation,
Dinard
1999
oil on canvas
150 x 150 cm
The Artist

and orange. These flat planes are contrasted by controlled areas of pattern and a textural application of paint. Her preoccupation with sgraffito marks into the surface of the wet oil paint and the intricate brushwork that describes the delicate patterns of crochet shawls, cardigans, tablecloths and bed linen has been consistent (Plate 26). Her initial interest in pattern began as a very young school girl following exercises set by Marion Richardson's book *Writing and Writing Patterns* (University of London Press 1935). The pattern is also the result of her love of weaving and textiles.

These are interiors that are lived in, littered with coffee cups, half-eaten croissants and used table napkins (Plate 24). With a flattening of the spatial relationships and oblique perspective,

39.
Bathers and Joggers at Tenby
1999
oil on canvas
150 x 150 cm
The Artist

her preoccupied subjects are caught adopting distracted awkward poses. There is more movement in these works than in the earlier, static paintings. The seriousness of the activities and their relevance to the artist ensure that the paintings are not sentimental.

The paintings have significance beyond the sitting room, bedroom, kitchen or bathroom. Williams uses the human figure as metaphor; as a personification of 'motherhood' or vehicle for abstract concepts. Her grandchildren and other family members have now replaced her own children as models, nevertheless Williams has remained steadfast in her treatment of the subject. The paintings are derived from observation and her family experiences but her figures are not portraits. The act of recording appearance is secondary to Williams' endeavour to suggest physical types. She is a keen observer of human relationships and endeavours to evoke inner feeling through outer form and record it with integrity and insight (Plate 29). Surprisingly Williams' diminutive stature does not at all match the boldness and physical presence of her paintings, or the monumental rounded forms of the female bodies that dominate her large canvases.

Williams gives the impression that she works without the subject's knowledge and arranges the pose to appear unstaged, casual or spontaneous. Life is contained within the canvas, the mother is concerned for her child alone, the little girls play unselfconsciously with one another, and lovers are totally absorbed in their moment together. No one looks out from the canvas to engage us or to invite a gaze. We are the onlookers because life within the picture is so totally self-contained, Williams considers only the interaction between her subjects and their environment. The subjects of *On the Sand* (1987), *The Shell* (1992) and *Conversation, Dinard* (1999) are unaware of being observed, mothers relax in the sun as they keep a weather-eye on their children absorbed in play (Plates 27, 33, 38). The preoccupied 'only child', never too far from its mother, is a pertinent theme for Williams who is all too familiar with the child's activities and fantasies as he or she 'passes time' without a playmate. These families are relaxed, semi-clothed, amidst the paraphernalia of beach holidays: bathing costumes, baskets, towels, wind breaks, beach shoes and the ubiquitous bucket and spade.

> Many a time I have sat on a crowded beach in summertime while numerous families around me have lazed in the sun or splashed in the sea or built sandcastles. While everyone has been thus absorbed in his or her own occupation of the moment, I have been totally fascinated and absorbed in watching them. I study them closely and make swift sketches to capture what they are doing and then, as soon as they spot me and become embarrassed or maybe even annoyed, I have to quickly stop and conceal my work.[13]

In her paintings of mothers with their babies, bathers on the beach and musicians at rehearsal Williams captures attitudes and gestures that are unique to those activities. Her portrayal of maternity and motherhood, and the recurrent theme of domestic interiors and family life are a positive reaffirmation of the European figurative tradition. In this tradition pictures tell stories and the figures are made to 'speak' through the way they are arranged, or posed. In Williams' paintings we recognise a specific gesture or detail; gestures and actions have to be deciphered in order to read the story. These are private moments that we are privileged to share.

---

13. CW, *Caernarfon Herald* 11 September 1981.

Principal Exhibitions

Solo, two-person with Gwilym Prichard and selected group shows. The number of works
Claudia Williams exhibited has been indicated in brackets where the information is available.

1949
National Exhibition of Children's Art (First Prizewinner) (touring) (6)

1950
National Exhibition of Children's Art (touring)

1952
Portmadoc Arts and Crafts Exhibition (4)
National Eisteddfod of Wales

1953
Society for Education through Art (touring)
North Wales Group, First Annual Exhibition (touring) (2)
Portmadoc Arts and Crafts Exhibition (2)

1955
Portmadoc Arts and Crafts Exhibition (3)
National Eisteddfod of Wales (2)

1956
National Eisteddfod of Wales (2)

1957
Welsh Arts Council at Heals Art Gallery, London
Contemporary Welsh Painting and Sculpture (Arts Council/National Museum of Wales) (2)
Portmadoc Arts and Crafts Exhibition, Portmeirion (10)
National Eisteddfod of Wales (Highly Commended) (3)

1958
Welsh Names in Painting, Howard Roberts Gallery, Cardiff (8)
Society for Education through Art (touring)
Contemporary Welsh Painting and Sculpture (Arts Council) (2)
Contemporary Welsh Painting, Howard Roberts Gallery, Cardiff
Portmadoc Arts and Crafts Exhibition (6)
National Eisteddfod of Wales (Runner Up: Gold Medal) (3)
Royal Cambrian Academy, Conwy

1959
University of Wales, Bangor Arts Festival (with GP and Anthony Stevens) (31)
Society for Education through Art (touring) (3)
Howard Roberts Gallery, Cardiff (with GP, Jonah Jones and Selwyn Jones)
Portmeirion Group, Portmadoc
Autumn Collection, Howard Roberts Gallery, Cardiff (4)
Royal Cambrian Academy, Conwy

1960
National Eisteddfod of Wales

1961
Society for Education through Art (touring)
Spring Exhibition of Painting and Drawing, Howard Roberts Gallery, Cardiff (2)

1963
Royal Cambrian Academy, Conwy (2)
National Eisteddfod of Wales (Highly Commended) (2)
Bangor Art Gallery (7)

1964
Royal Cambrian Academy, Conwy (2)
Blue Coat Chambers, Liverpool (with GP) (21)
Old Town Hall, Criccieth (with GP and Kyffin Williams)

1965
Bangor Art Gallery (with GP)

1966
North Wales Artists, David Griffiths Gallery, Cardiff

1968
Paintings and Drawings, Tegfryn Art Gallery, Menai Bridge, Anglesey (solo)

1971
South Wales Arts Association
Tegfryn Art Gallery, Menai Bridge, Anglesey (with GP)

1972
Tegfryn Art Gallery, Menai Bridge, Anglesey (solo)

1974
Llangefni County Library, Anglesey (with GP) (20)

1975
Spring Exhibition, Albany Gallery, Cardiff
Royal Cambrian Academy, Conwy
Mid Wales House Gallery, Newbridge-on-Wye (with GP) (21)

1976
City Art Gallery, Hereford (with GP)
Christmas Exhibition, Albany Gallery, Cardiff

1978
Royal Cambrian Academy, Conwy (3)
South Wales Arts Association
City Art Gallery, Hereford (with GP)
Tegfryn Art Gallery, Menai Bridge, Anglesey (with GP) (21)
University of Wales, Gregynog Hall, Newtown (with GP)

1979
Royal Cambrian Academy, Conwy (6)
Tegfryn Art Gallery, Menai Bridge, Anglesey (with GP)
Madley Festival, Herefordshire

1980
Royal Cambrian Academy, Conwy (2)

1981
Royal Cambrian Academy, Conwy (3)
Holyhead Arts Festival (solo)
Through Artist's Eyes, Mostyn Art Gallery, Llandudno
Tegfryn Art Gallery, Menai Bridge, Anglesey (with GP) (36)
Places and People, Holyhead Library (with GP)

1982
Royal West of England Academy, Bristol

1983
Royal West of England Academy, Bristol
Wales, Wales, Wales, Arts Council/National Museum of Wales, Cardiff (touring)

1984
The Artist's Eye III, Mostyn Art Gallery, Llandudno
Royal West of England Academy, Bristol
Paintings and Drawings, Oriel 31, Welshpool (solo)

1985
Women's Art in Wales, Mostyn Art Gallery, Llandudno
National Museum of Wales (Turner House), Penarth (touring) (with GP)
Claudia Williams and Gwilym Prichard, Oriel Theatr Clwyd, Mold (40)
Hotel de Ville, St Maximin la Ste Baume in the Var, Provence (with GP)

1987
Salon de Nantes Biennale

1988
Forum International, Nantes (with GP and Ceri Pritchard)

1989
Ceri Richards Gallery, University of Wales, Swansea (with GP and Ben Pritchard)
Centre de Roger Portugal, University of Nantes (with GP)
Nantes Biennale
Salon de Vannes (First prizewinner)
Credit Agricol Bank, Vannes
Salon d'Autumne, Paris
Galerie Romanet, Rue de Seine, Paris (solo)

1990
A Woman's View, Heffer Gallery, Cambridge (6)
Espace Paul Gauguin, Pont Aven, Brittany (solo)
Foundation Paul Ricard, Paris (solo)
Beaumaris Arts Festival (2 person)
Galerie Hoche, Vannes (solo)

1991
Foundation Paul Ricard, Paris
Domaine de Trevarez Cultural Centre, Quimper, Finistere (solo)
Oriel Plas Glyn y Weddw, Llanbedrog (with GP) (31)

1992
Galerie Moyon-Avenard, Nantes (solo)
Galerie Van Hove, Quimper (solo)
Galerie Saphir, Dinard (with GP)

1993
Galerie Saphir, Paris (with GP)
Beaux Arts, Paris salon (elected Member)

1994
Espace Paul Gauguin, Pont Aven, Brittany
Galerie L'Atelier, Angers (with GP)
Galerie Saphir, Dinard, Becherel and Paris (with GP)
Philip Mouwes Gallery, Amsterdam (solo)

1995

Travelling Together – Paintings 1985-1995, Oriel Ynys Môn, Anglesey (with GP)
Attic Gallery, Swansea (with GP)
Summer Exhibition, Martin Tinney Gallery, Cardiff
Galerie Moyon-Avenard, Nantes (solo)
Galerie Alpha, Le Havre
Galerie Saphir, Dinard (with GP)
Nationa Library of Wales, Aberystwyth, 'William Mathias'
Travelling Together, New Paintings, Attic Gallery, Swansea (with GP) (25)

1996

The Fort, Ste. Marine, Benodet (Retrospective) (with GP, Ceri and Ben Pritchard)
Galerie Saphir, Dinard (with GP)
Galerie Van Hove, Quimper (solo)
Summer Exhibition, Martin Tinney Gallery, Cardiff
Galerie Alpha, Le Havre

1997

New Paintings, Martin Tinney Gallery, Cardiff (with GP)
New Work, Attic Gallery, Swansea (with GP)
Book Gallery, St Ives
50 Years of the Contemporary Art Society for Wales, National Museum of Wales (touring)
Winter Exhibition, Martin Tinney Gallery, Cardiff

1998

People and Places, Museum of Modern Art, Machynlleth (with GP)
People and Places, University of Wales, Gregynog (with GP)

1999

New Paintings, Martin Tinney Gallery, Cardiff (with GP)
Site de la Canterie, St Fiacre-sur-Maine (with GP)
Galerie Van Hove, Quimper (solo)
Galerie Yves Halter, Rennes
Galerie Moyon-Avenard, Nantes (with GP)

2000

A Retrospective, National Library of Wales, Aberystwyth
Works on Paper (A Retrospective), University of Wales, Aberystwyth, School of Art
Summer Exhibition, Martin Tinney Gallery

Public Collections

Arts Council of Wales
Bodley Head Publishers, London
Cardiff Education Authority
Cassells Publishers, London
Clwyd Education Authority
Contemporary Art Society for Wales
Gwent Education Authority
Gwynedd Education Authority
Hereford City Art Gallery
Hôtel de Region, Nantes
Marks and Spencer Ltd
National Library of Wales, Aberystwyth
North Wales Arts Association
Newport Art Gallery
Southampton City Art Gallery
University of Wales, Aberystwyth
University of Wales, Bangor
University of Wales, Cardiff

Select Bibliography, Exhibition Reviews and Magazine Articles

I was fortunate to have access to Claudia Williams' file of press reviews (not all of which it has been possible to identify, and some references are incomplete), magazine articles, exhibition catalogues and flyers. Contributions to exhibitions were also to be found in catalogues for Contemporary Welsh Painting and Sculpture, Royal Cambrian Academy, Portmadoc Arts Club, North Wales Group, North Wales Arts Association, Young Welsh Artists, Howard Roberts Gallery, Society for Education through Art and the National Eisteddfod of Wales.

'National Exhibition of Children's Art', *Sunday Pictorial,* 5 June 1949

'Caterham Girls Scoop Art Contest', *Coulsdon and Purley Times and Surrey County Mail,* 16 July 1949

Cambrian News, 29 July 1949

'National Exhibition of Children's Art', *The School Master and Woman Teacher's Chronicle,* 4 August 1949

'Minister Praises the Work of 272 Boy and Girl Artists', *Sunday Pictorial,* 4 September 1949

'£250 Art Grant for Caterham Girl', *The Purley and Coulsdon Advertiser,* 9 September 1949

'A Child's Academy', *The Times Educational Supplement,* 9 September 1949

'Claudia, £250 Training Grant Winner, Shows Her Work to Minister', *Coulsdon and Purley Times,* 9 September 1949

'National Exhibition of Children's Art', *The Listener,* 15 September 1949

Patrick Heron, 'Children's Paintings', *The New Statesman and Nation,* 17 September 1949

'Ysgoloriaeth', *Y Cymro* 24 September 1949

Leader Magazine, 10 December 1949

R R Tomlinson, *Picture and Pattern-Making by Children,* Studio, London

Jonah Jones, 'The Art of Gwilym Pritchard and Claudia Williams' *Anglo-Welsh Review* Vol.11, No.27 1958

'Ammanford's Eisteddfod Success', *Manchester Guardian,* August 1958

Goronwy Powell, 'It's Art in a Council House for Two', August 1958

Ellis Gwyn Jones, 'Yr Arddangosfa Gelfyddyd', *Baner ac Amserau Cymru,* August 1958

Colm Trevor, 'Colourful Paintings from the North', *Western Mail,* 7 March 1959

Goronwy Powell 'Happy Ending to Six Months Hard Labour', *Western Mail* 11 March 1959

'Five Young Artists', *Liverpool Daily Post,* April 1959

'A Glimpse of Art in Wales', *Caernarvon and Denbigh Herald,* 27 November 1959

Sion Daniel, *Gwilym Prichard and Claudia Williams,* Bluecoat Chambers, Liverpool 1964, 6pp

"Z", 'Two Artists Free of Artifice', Liverpool 1964

'Gwynedd Artists to the Fore', 1964

M G McNay, 'Exhibitions at Wrexham', 5 January 1965

'Artists in North Wales', *Architecture Wales,* Cardiff May-June 1967

'Artist Mother Stages Her First Solo Exhibition', 7 May 1969

'After the Children are Put to Bed', *Liverpool Daily Post,* 1969

J Herington, 'Pictures with Real Feeling', *Portraits and Heads* at Hereford c.1975

'Talented Couple Settle in County', Hereford, July 1975

'Claudia Williams – Portrait Painter', *Herefordshire Life,* March 1976, pp.5-8

Bedwyr Lewis Jones, 'Gwledd o Luniau Lliwgwar a Llawen', June 1978

Sheila Mackenzie, *Paintings and Drawings by Gwilym Prichard and Claudia Williams* Tegfryn Art Gallery, Anglesey, September 1981, 6pp

Elizabeth Carter, 'Her Work Depicts the Unexpected', *Caernarvon and Denbigh Herald,* 11 September 1981

'William Mathias', BBC Wales Documentary featuring Williams' portrait of the composer

William Mathias, 'Ave Rex, Elegy for a Prince etc', Lyrita Records, Williams' portrait on the CD cover

'Eisteddfod Memories', *Liverpool Daily Post,* 21 February 1983

Simond Liddell, 'A Lyrical Response', *Link,* March 1983, p.11

Hywel Harries, *Cymru'r Cynfas,* Y Lolfa, Aberystwyth 1984

Moira Vincentelli, *Women's Art in Wales,* Mostyn Art Gallery, 1985, p.8

Kate Nicholas, 'Women's Art in Wales', (review) 1985

Kristel Schwartz, 'Deux Peintres du Pays de Galles', *Var Martin,* 26 June 1985

'Art on Show', *The Journal,* 31 October 1985

'Contrasting Choice of Painting Pair', *The Chronicle,* 1 November 1985

Moira Vincentelli, 'Women Painters of Traditional Subjects' *Feminist Art News* Vol. 2, No.4, pp.6-8

G R Owen, 'A Place in the Gallery for Artists from France', *Caernarfon Herald,* 3 April 1987

'Claudia Williams – Les Oeuvres Aident L'esprit', *Ouest France,* 22 November 1988

Planet No.69, June/July 1988 (painting reproduced on the back cover)

'Exposition des Oeuvres de Claudia Williams', *L'Avenir,* 3 November 1989

'La Chaleur de Claudia Williams', *La Liberté,* 8 November 1989

'Claudia Williams, Fidèle à Elle-Mème', *La Liberté,* 28 November 1990

'Claudia Williams, Premier Prix du Salon des Peintres', *La Liberté,* 25 January 1989

Acwila Williams, 'Artist with a Vision', 1991

'Pier le Basque, Claudia Williams l'Anglaise et Louis Suire, le Rochelais', *Telegramme,* 30 January 1991

'L'exposition Des Peintures de Pier, Williams et Suire est Ouverte', *Telegramme,* 2 February 1991

'Vernissage d'une Triple Exposition', *Telegramme du Breste,* 5 February 1991

'Trois Peintres au Style Differént', *Ouest-France,* 16 February 1991

JP Le Marc, 'Exposition Pier, Suire, Williams', 16 March 1991

'Claudia Williams', *Expositions Trevarez,* Saint-Goazec 1991, pp.14-21

'Claudia Williams', *Tout Prévoir* No.225, October 1991

Alain Farelle, 'Claudia Williams, Mère a L'enfant', *Presse Ocean,* 3 December 1991

Nicola Heywood Thomas, 'Artists Abroad', *Primetime,* HTV Wales, 30-minute documentary 1991

Rhys Lewis, *Gwilym Prichard,* Hel Steon, Television 1991

Daniel Morvan, 'Claudia Williams – Des Femmes sur La Plage', *Ouest France,* 11 April 1992

'Claudia Williams – Une Anglaise sur le Continent', *Telegramme,* 4 May 1992

Francine Szapiro (interview), *Gwilym Prichard and Claudia Williams,* Radio Paris, 18 March 1993

'Prichard et Williams à la Galerie Saphir', *Ouest France,* 18 September 1994

'Attic Gallery', *Art Review* April 1995 p.63

Sharen Griffith, 'Arlunwyr Teithiol yn Dychwelyd i Fôn', *Yr Herald,* 18 March 1995

Ian Skidmore, *Wales on Sunday,* 19 March 1995

Roger Gicquel, 'En Flanant en Bretagne', Television France 3, 1995

Keith Harrison 'Travelling Together with Memories in Oil', *The Mail,* 22 March 1995

Celia Lucas, 'Have Paint Box Will Travel', *Liverpool Daily Post,* 4 April 1995

Ian Skidmore, 'Claudia Williams and Gwilym Prichard, Travelling Together', BBC Radio Wales, 30-minute interview, May 1995

Alain Favelle, 'Claudia Williams Mère a L'Enfant'

'Gwilym Prichard and Claudia Williams Exposent', *Ouest France,* 17 August 1995

'Gathering of the Llans', *Hampstead and Highgate Times,* 15 March 1996

Peter Wakelin 'Focus on Wales', *Art Review,* October 1997, p.66

Robert Meyrick, 'People and Places', Museum of Modern Art, Wales 1998, 4pp

David Buckman, *Dictionary of Artists in Britain since 1945,* Art Dictionaries, London 1998, p.1280

'Showcase Wales', *Modern Painters,* Summer 1998, p.96

Rhyddid y Nofel (book cover), University of Wales Press, Cardiff 1999

David Gauduchn-Granse (ed.), 'Claudia Williams and Gwilym Prichard' *Practique des Arts,* July 2000, 8pp